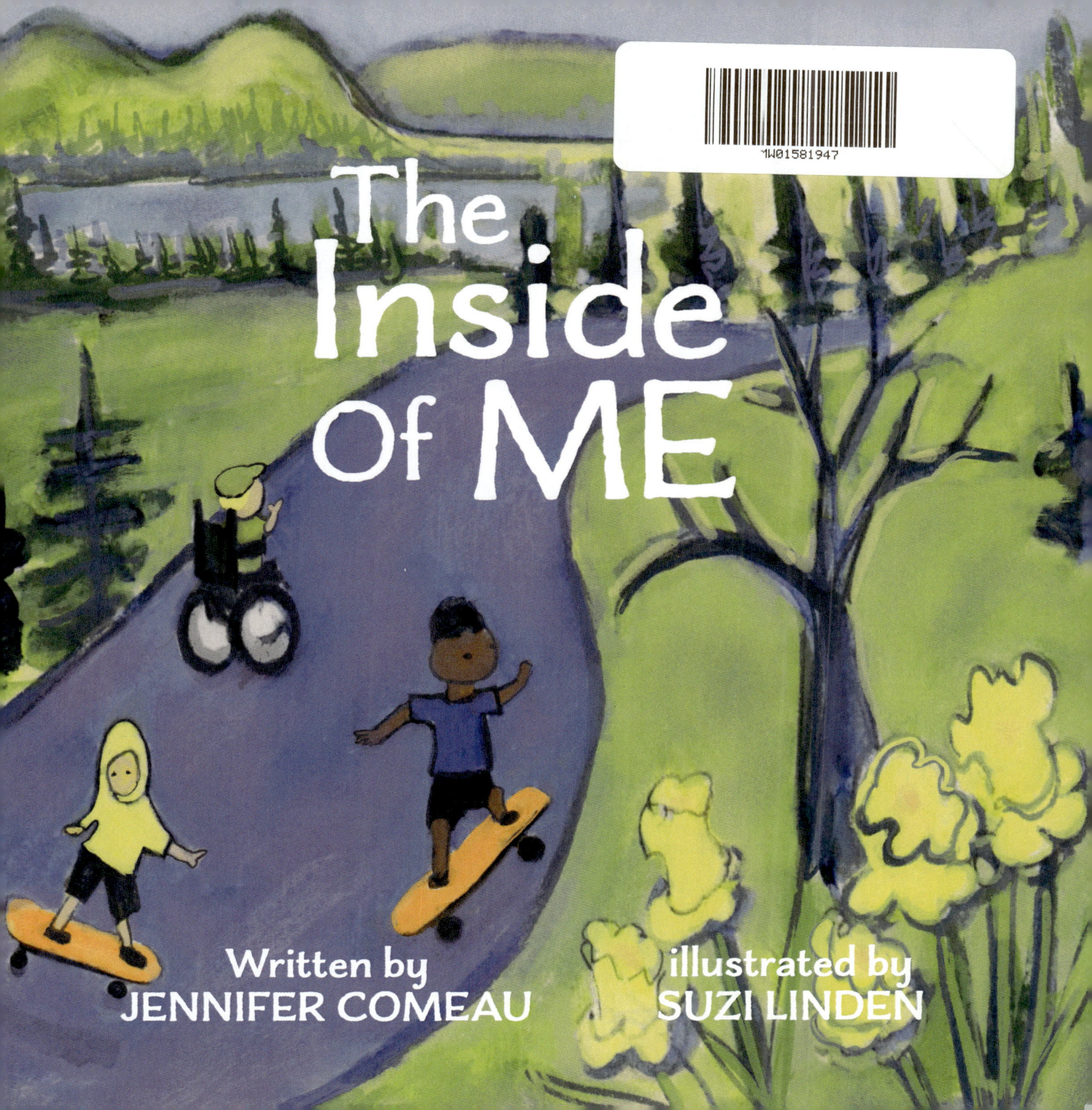

The Inside of ME

Written by JENNIFER COMEAU

illustrated by SUZI LINDEN

Copyright © 2024 by Jennifer Comeau
First Edition — 2024

All rights reserved.

No part of this publication may be reproduced in any form, or by any means, electronic or mechanical, including photocopying, recording, or any information browsing, storage, or retrieval system, without permission in writing from the author and publisher.
www.jennifercomeau.com

Illustrated by Suzi Linden | www.suzilinden.com
Interior and Cover Design: Mariella Travis | www.alleiram.com

ISBN
978-1-961905-25-2 (Hardcover)
978-1-961905-14-6 (Paperback)
978-1-961905-15-3 (eBook)

12 Willows Press
Winterport, Maine
www.12willowspress.com

With deepest gratitude, I dedicate this book to soil and sea, feathers and forests, mica and mountains, and every being who calls Earth home; to Julia O'Hara, who helped immeasurably; for John Comeau, always. -- JC

To the chickadees outside my window and the woodpecker laughing from the tree and to all the artists with worlds inside their skull waiting to be free. -- SL

who fly, swim, or hop
while I perch on a rock?

Is there a hill I can climb for a vista sublime?

So go find a place on a sun-shiny day.

Or float on a swell, be a seal or a fish.

Go outside where Awe and Wonder reside.
Let the magic of nature...

Featured Places In Maine

1. Pondicherry Park, Bridgton

Pondicherry Park is 66 acres of woodlands, wetlands, and fields in the heart of downtown Bridgton. It features 2 miles of walking trails and a new 0.7-mile-long universal access trail. The park has numerous boardwalks, an amphitheater, and multiple bridges spanning the brooks. Wildlife includes barred owls, loons, mallards, Northern cardinals, and many of Maine's wildlife creatures.

Invitation: Trees as Listeners

Some people think trees are great listeners. While visiting Pondicherry Park, wander the woods and look at the trees. Is there one that grabs your attention? Study its unique shape, touch, and scent. Do you have a secret to share with the tree?

2. Jasper Beach, Machiasport

Jasper Beach in Howard Cove was named after the attractive red volcanic stones that cover the beach. Called rhyolite, the stones have a polished surface formed by constant abrasion from water and sand. At the beach's eastern edge, a freshwater inlet drains from a salt marsh into the sea. The water in the inlet teems with rock crabs while migratory birds roam the beach.

Invitation: Romancing the Stone

Jasper Beach is also known for its "singing" stones, which clatter against each other as the tide ebbs and flows. Find a spot to sit and let your eyes be drawn to a stone. Hold it in your hands. Press it to your heart. Study the stone's shape, color, weight, and texture. How does holding it make you feel?

3. Jordan Pond, Mount Desert Island

Jordan Pond is located within Acadia National Park on Mount Desert Island. Steep mountainsides border the pond's shores that overlook the Bubbles and the Pemetic Mountain. Lake trout, salmon, mergansers, loons, tadpoles, and frogs call this special place home. Near dawn or dusk, you may discover North American beavers, whose lodges are visible from the trail.

Invitation: To be a Water Creature

As you meander the trail along Jordan Pond, find a spot to pause and notice the water's movement and how it shifts and changes from one place to the next. What would it feel like to be a little fish swimming with the current, a frog floating in the water, or a beaver building a dam?

4. Mount Agamenticus, Ogunquit

With its 10,000-plus acres of forest, this mountain supports many animal and plant species. Highbush blueberries, shagbark hickory, chestnut oak, Atlantic white cedar swamp, hemlock, and black gum trees grow along one of the mountain's former ski slopes. Snowshoe hares, wild turkeys, and great horned owls call this place home. The wetlands and vernal pools surrounding Mount Agamenticus serve as breeding and feeding grounds for wood frogs, blue-spotted salamanders, spotted and Blanding's turtles, and ebony- and ringed-boghaunter dragonflies. Cars are allowed up the mountain, where the Big A trail has universal access and its own viewing platform so everyone can see the sights.

Invitation: Skywatching

Mount Agamenticus has grassy places near its peak. Find a place to lie or sit down. Look up at the sky. What do you see?

5. Peaks-Kenny State Park, Dover-Foxcroft

Peaks-Kenny State Park borders the southern shore of Sebec Lake, offering nearly 900 acres of peaceful woodland for boating, fishing, swimming, hiking, and picnicking. The park has 10 miles of hiking trails for visitors of all ages and skill levels. Day visitors and campers can enjoy old-growth hardwood forests, hemlock, and pines. The park is home to many mushrooms and to wildlife like deer, songbirds, chipmunks, and squirrels. A notable landmark along the lake is the "Castle," a shorefront home built in 1890 by a Foxcroft attorney.

Invitation: Earthen Living Room

As you wander the trails, look for a space that calls to you, something that looks like a little living room. What would it feel like to explore the earthen living room?

6. Bald Mountain, Rangeley

Despite lacking wheelchair accessibility, this mountain offers panoramic views of Rangeley, Cupsuptic, and Mooselookmeguntic Lakes, Maine's Saddleback and Elephant Mountains, and New Hampshire's Mount Washington. A trail winds through northern hardwood trees, leading to a summit with scrubby red spruce and bare granite. At the top, visitors can find an observation tower and picnic tables. The area is abundant with spruce grouse, gray jay, boreal chickadees, and blackpoll warblers.

Invitation: Treasure Seeking

Picture this place as a treasure waiting for you, waiting to be found by your heart. Follow your feet and senses to uncover it. Maybe it's something you can hold, a word that comes to mind, or even a sighting of a creature.

7. Katahdin Woods and Waters National Monument, Stacyville

The Katahdin Woods and Waters National Monument invites discovery of its rivers, streams, woods, flora, fauna, geology, and night skies that have fascinated humans for millennia. The Penobscot East Branch flows over rocks dating back 500 million years, with signs of ancient coral reefs. Moose, black bears, river otters, and the elusive Canada lynx live here, as do frogs, hawks, ducks, salamanders, bald eagles, and whip-poor-wills.

Invitation: Color Gazing

As you travel through Katahdin Woods and Waters, let your eyes lead you on an exploration of color. What colors are you drawn to? How many shades of greens and grays can you find?

8. Goose Rocks Beach, Kennebunkport

This 2.5-mile-long natural landscape features three sweeping crescents of dove-gray sand, dune grasses, and rocky islands accessible at low tide. The beach is a habitat for endangered piping plovers, many shorebirds, and seals resting on rock outcroppings.

Invitation: Screach-Squeeking Your Way

While visiting Goose Rocks Beach, notice the distinctive sound you hear when walking quickly across the sand. What does it sound like?

9. Musquash Esker Trail, Talmadge

The Musquash Esker Trail, located roughly 5.5 miles east of Grand Lake Stream, offers an ADA-accessible trail suitable for wheelchairs and strollers. It has wildlife like songbirds, turtles, and beavers, as well as plants, mushrooms, and a diverse tree canopy. Rare sights of black bears and coyotes are possible. In the winter, it's a great spot for cross-country skiing. The trail, spanning 1.4 miles (2.8 miles round-trip), leads to Big Musquash Stream, where a viewing platform offers gorgeous views of Amazon Mountain and over 5,000 acres of pristine wetlands. Informational signs along the trail provide insights into the area's glacial, ecological, and logging history.

Invitation: If in Winter

Winter snow provides a unique opportunity to find animal prints. As you walk the trail, what prints do you come across? Big prints, like a bear's or coyote's? Tiny prints, like a mouse's or squirrel's? Can you identify the prints you see?

Invitation: If at Sunset

As the sun sets, watch its movement and colors and the sounds of the landscape. Can you hear birds making their last calls before going to sleep? How do the colors shift as daylight fades into darkness?

MAP YOUR FAVORITE PLACE

Draw a map of your neighborhood, state, province, or country on the following pages. Mark places on it that you want to explore—maybe a big tree to picnic beneath, a garden to wander, a hill to climb, or a water source to visit.

When you finally arrive at one of the spots, imagine melting into the landscape. What happens with all your senses? What faraway sounds can you hear? What does the place feel like? What scents tickle your nose? Notice the play of sunlight and shadows. If you had to choose two or three words to describe the place, what would they be?

Take a photo and email it along with your short description to wildwonder@jennifercomeau.com. Select photos may be used in workshops, social media, and talks; if yours is chosen, you will be given credit!

ABOUT THE AUTHOR

JENNIFER COMEAU treasures walks in Maine's special woodland places. A Certified Forest Therapy Guide, singer-songwriter, and author-speaker, Jen's experiences among "the standing ones" are awe-inspiring and grounding. Her forthcoming debut novel, *A Moon in All Things* (12 Willows Press, 2025), is a heroine's journey to reclaim the old ways of nature. As a trustee for TreeSisters.org, an international reforestation and women's leadership organization, she lives with her husband, Lt. Col. John Comeau, and a spunky poodle, Bridey, in Kennebunkport, Maine. Find Jen at: www.jennifercomeau.com.

ABOUT THE ILLUSTRATOR

SUZI LINDEN is a lifelong artist who translates her joy of nature into her work. She is the author-illustrator of three *Princess Bigfoot* books—*Princess Bigfoot in Alaska* (2022), *Princess Bigfoot Gives Thanks* (2023), and *Princess Bigfoot in Maine* (2023)—by Linden Press Publishing. She lives in western Maine, where she works and wanders her trails for daily inspiration. Find Suzi at: www.suzilinden.com.

Made in United States
Orlando, FL
27 June 2024

48361630R00024